The Issue Is YOU

One-on-One with YourSELF

A. B. Almore

The Issue Is YOU

One-on-One with YourSELF

Published By:
AB Publishing
P.O Box 14520
New Bern NC 28561

www.abalmore.com

Copyright © 2010 A.B. Almore
Interior Text Design by Pamela S. Almore
Cover Design by Pamela S. Almore of Omni Print Co.
ISBN: 978-1-4536780-7-7

First Edition
Printed and bound in the United States of America by AB Publishing
www.abalmore.com

Dedication

This book is dedicated to my Pastor, John H. Pierce Jr., and Elder, Judy Pierce, of St. John Missionary Baptist Church. Your teachings and lifestyles inspired me to confront my issues within. For that, I'm eternally grateful. God bless you!

Contents

I Dare You

Don't even think about it. I know when you saw the cover of this book, read the title, and skimmed over the back, immediately somebody else's face popped into your mind. "Hmm, this will be a good book for So-and-So to read. This is exactly what they need to get themselves together."

Well, I've got news for you. When God placed this book in my spirit, I didn't have "So-and-So" in mind. I had your face in mind! I had your insecurities, your weaknesses, your internal thoughts and wars in mind—the side of you that nobody knows about. Oh, you know what I'm talking about—the side of you that curses your spouse out in your mind daily. *Careful! It's only a matter of time until it manifests outwardly.*

The Other You

I thought about the side of you that you throw into the closet when your Pastor and other tiers of leadership come around. I want to speak to the part of you that's afraid to do what God is calling you to do. This is for the one who's behind the mask that you put on before walking out of the house. By the way, you forgot to put your mask on one morning. Everybody knows you're fronting!

It's OK though—nobody's around but you and me. Just keep reading. It's time to address those wounds. It's time to confront those pains and to bring those disappointments and failures out of the closet.

It's Now or Never

It's time for you to get a grip on your emotions and stop passing the blame on to your children, to your spouse, and to your co-workers. It's time for you to embrace the one thing that you have neglected for years now—the mirror of reality.

All these years you have looked in the mirror, but you have looked past yourself. When is the last time you stared into your own eyes and dealt with yourself? Do you even know what you look like anymore? You're so fierce and quick to jump on others who are on the outside, but cowardly enough to look past the one on the inside.

Deal with Yourself

You, my friend, are your worst enemy. You are the weakest link in your life. You are a walking excuse and a brilliant blamer. You have been delivered from so many things. Now it's time for the greatest deliverance of all— the deliverance from self! You have been waiting for this moment your whole life, but you didn't have the heart to deal with yourself.

These next couple of pages are going to be brutal yet truthful. I dare you to clear your mind of your spouse, your children, church, friends, family, and co-workers. Politely ask them to exit your mind. This time, it's personal. This time, your energy, focus, and rage aren't channeled toward them. They're channeled toward yourself. I dare you to be real, to be honest, and to be sincere. I dare you to deal with yourself!

Nathan

Then Nathan said to David, "You are the man!"
2 Samuel 12:7

Look at you! What in the world happened to you? How did you manage to get so far off track? How did you allow yourself to become so negative? What happened to the boundaries in your life? I don't see any self-control. Just look at your eating and spending habits. Something has gone terribly wrong!

Not only that, but there aren't any signs of righteousness in your life. You're full of excuses. You're shaping the Gospel to fit your lifestyle. You're depressed. You're blaming others. You have made a complete mess of your life. But how did it get to this? I know what happened. You never had a true Nathan.

Two Types

Notice I said "a true Nathan." There are two types of Nathans. One Nathan tells you, "You are the man!" Then you have the second Nathan that tells you, "You are the man!" You need both, but without the other, your life will be unbalanced. *A false balance is an abomination unto the Lord* (Proverbs 11:1). You have had the former Nathan but lacked the latter. Allow me to explain.

The former Nathan smacked you on your back and told you that you were all that. He constantly built your ego up. He constantly encouraged and praised your strong points. As the author of *Risk* puts it, you had fans, but you never had friends! Fans will tell you what you want to hear instead of what you need to hear.

Fans

I remember standing outside at a college football game. The team had just blown a major lead and lost the game. The fans were outside waiting for them to pat them on the back, to tell them "Good job," to tell them to hang in there and not to worry about it! But that's what fans do. They often tell you what you want to hear, but you need more than that.

That night, that team played horribly. They needed to know where they messed up so that they could correct the issue. What those fans should've said was, "Come on, guys; what happened? How in the world did you blow a 17-point lead? You failed to execute; you failed to capitalize. You got tired in the fourth quarter. You're out of shape; you quit playing. You know you're better than that. Go back to the drawing board and get it together!"

Your life is similar to that team. You were up at one point, but you've blown the lead! You have failed to execute and capitalize the blessings of God. You have gotten weary, and you've given up too fast. You let go of your health. There's no balance to your diet. You gave up on life, you gave up on your family, but, most of all, you gave up on yourself! But the problem is that—you have fans in your ear and not true friends.

Friends

Friends will look you in the eye and tell you everything that I just said. They will let you know when you need a Tic-Tac. They will let you know when your dress is too tight and when you need to lose some weight. They will let you know when you're out of line. And, most importantly, they will let you know when they see pride kicking in. They will address your fears, your weaknesses, and your insecurities. They will tell you the truth. Even though it hurts, you will thank them later.

> *He who rebukes a man will find more favor afterward*
> *than he who flatters with the tongue.*
> Proverbs 28:23

Get away from people that always flatter, and get around somebody that can tell you the truth! You need the latter Nathans in your life—the ones that won't flatter you but instead tell it like it is. They will be there to tell you that you are the man that you feared to become!

They will let you know that the very one that you once despised, you have now become. Real Nathans get in your face when everyone is talking about you behind your back. They tell you the truth; they tell you, "Thus says the Lord." They let you take it however you want.

The Missing Ingredient

This is what's been missing from your life, the truth—the up-close and personal truth. The real Nathans have been missing, and all you have been receiving is pats on the back, telling you "Good job." I'm not here for that. Go somewhere else if you're looking for sympathy because this isn't the book! Do you not know that *open rebukes are better than hidden love*? (Proverbs 27:5)

David was at a place in life where he was at a standstill. The prophet came and told David a parable about a wealthy man who became greedy and took from one that had less than he. David burned with anger when he heard the parable.

David despised the man in the parable and said that he deserved death! Nathan looked him in the eye and said, "It's you! You are the man that I'm talking about." Nathan left David with no choice but to deal with himself.

The Difference

Now, what makes David different from you is that he faced his issues, but you don't. David didn't get offended, but you do. David didn't buck against what he said. He didn't deny the fact. He didn't make any excuses. He simply said to Nathan, "I have sinned against the Lord." That one-letter word held the bulk of his deliverance: "I." David simply said, "It's me, Lord. It's me, standing in the need of prayer."

David could've easily passed the blame. He could've easily had Nathan killed. He was the King, you know. He could've gotten defensive and said, "Who do you think you *are*, getting in my face? I'm the King. I could have you killed!" Instead, David humbled himself, searched his heart, and began to confront his issues.

God Sent

Of all the great things the Lord did in David's life, I believe the greatest can be found in 2 Samuel 12:1. It reads, *"The Lord sent Nathan to David."* The Lord sent Nathan to help David get back on track. God didn't send a fan—he sent a friend. David didn't pick him, but the Lord sent him. Understand this. You will never pick a Nathan. The Lord has to send him.

If it was up to you, you would pick someone lesser than you who would never challenge your walk. You would never pick somebody greater than you to challenge your personal space. This is why God sends Nathans your way. He sends Nathans your way for you to get delivered so that you can get to the next level. Don't despise it. Don't reject it, and don't overlook it. This book is serious, and so is your destiny. It's time for you to face yourself!

Nathan

Your Latter Will Be Greater

For the next couple of chapters, I would like to be your Nathan. Get somewhere quiet, read this book, and examine yourself. The key to this book is acknowledging the issue. If you have to cry, go ahead and cry. When it's all said and done, I promise you that you will be a better person. Nathan wasn't sent to be David's fan, and I'm not either.

I imagine that David was embarrassed, upset, and offended. But he took heed, and from that point on, he became God's man. So you might be embarrassed, you might get upset and offended. But I really don't care. As long as I get you to that place in God where you're latter supersedes your former, then I have done my job.

And blessed is he who isn't offended because of me.
Matthew 11:6

New Mind Resolution

Be transformed by the renewing of the mind.
Romans 12:2 NIV

Today is December 26 and Christmas has already come and gone. The money has been spent, and the presents have been ripped open. Many parents and spouses are beating themselves up now for spending more money than they intended. Some spent tithe money, some spent bill money, but to say the least, they spent too much money. Through the rage of that gesture, one still finds hope. The New Year is almost here!

"I can put that on my New Year's Resolution. Save more money next year. Yeah, that's what I will do. I will save more money next year, plan for Christmas in advance, and stop eating out so much. Speaking of eating out, I will join the gym this year too, again. But this time I'm going to go twice a week—no, three times a week. As a matter of fact, I'm going to go before work. No, I mean after work. Yeah, that's what I will do!"

New Mind = Change

And with that reasoning, they feel better about themselves. How pathetic. Imagine that—a fresh start, clean slate, all because of a new year. New Year's resolutions—many make them, but how many keep them?

Think about it. After all those New Year's Resolutions that you have made over the last couple of years, have any of them been resolved? Nah, I didn't think so! Don't get mad at me. Get mad at yourself!

I have come to the conclusion that New Year's resolutions are a bunch of bologna. You don't need a New Year's resolution. What you need is a new mind resolution! I don't care what year it is and how many changes you have put down on paper. Until your mind changes, nothing is going to change!

Integrity

A new year with the same mind will produce the same results. You have to stop playing games with yourself. If you can't be real with yourself, you won't be real with others. Practice integrity with yourself first. Work on keeping your word with yourself, and you will be amazed at what happens.

Even if the job is cool, you don't have to be late. Your boss might not mind, but get back from lunch on time. Clock out when you're supposed to. If you're on salary, don't take advantage of the system. Focus on gaining personal victories in these areas, and they will be sure to usher you into the next level.

But it all starts with the mind. I know you think you know this Scripture, but that's the problem. You don't know this Scripture until you *become* this Scripture. Read it slowly, and allow it to sink into your spirit.

Do not conform any longer to the pattern of this world, but be transformed by the renewing of the mind.

Patterns

That verse is so powerful. I challenge you to chew on that text until you master it. Stop chasing fresh revelation until you put into practice your existing revelation. Let's pull some highlighted points out of that verse. The first thing I want to bring to your attention is "the pattern of this world." To get to the next level in life, you must break away from the patterns of this world.

I'm not talking about adultery, smoking, drinking, and fornication. You need to break away from those, too. But for the mature crowd, those might not be the issues.

The patterns that you must steer away from are blaming others, waiting on others, pity parties, and viewing everybody as a problem except yourself. These patterns have kept you from dealing with the real issue all of these years—you!!!

The word *patterns* can be defined in one single word, "behavior." The word *behavior* can singlehandedly be defined by the word *response*. You must stop behaving and responding like the world does. You are *in* the world, but not *of* the world.

You have to get to a place where you pull back and analyze yourself. Where did I go wrong? What did I say that triggered the argument? Did I do something to cause me to get fired? Learn to accept responsibility for your actions, words, and thoughts. But in order to do that, you must stop conforming to the patterns of this world. While the world passes the blame, you have to be the one to accept the blame!

Transform

The only way that you will not conform is to transform. I challenge you this very instant to transform right where you are: Geographically, mentally, spiritually, and socially. The old you doesn't exist anymore. Your old ways, your old reasoning, your old responses, and your old behavior are gone! *You* can transform in an instant, *you* can transfigure in the twinkling of an eye, but *you* have to want to!

The word *transform* means "to change, reform, alter, renovate." I give you permission to redefine yourself. Many of you have been waiting for somebody to release the new you that has been bound for years. There's a part of you that the world hasn't seen, heard, or embraced, and that you were afraid to release because of what others may say or think about you.

But truth be told, the world isn't against you. It's for you. But you are against yourself. The world has seen glimpses of that side of you here and there, but it is you who won't let that other side of you out. You're afraid to transform because you're conditioned to the pattern!

But what eagle doesn't soar, what 747 doesn't fly, and what child of God doesn't transform? Changing and shifting are part of your walk with God. It's exciting, it's innovating, it's mind blowing, and it's obtainable. Break away from those past wounds, shake off those disappointments, and divorce your insecurities instead of your husband or wife. Stand back and watch God blow your mind!

Mind Games

Speaking of the mind, that's where the trans-formation must start. The mind is made up of six major components. They are the **memory, imagination, perception, thoughts, will, and emotions.**

The mind is what you must guard with all of your heart. This is the place where you must be sober and vigilant because your adversary is looking for opportunities to place sensors inside your mind.

Once he has those sensors inside your mind, he can then control and program you from afar. Through pain, disappointments, and failures, you have given him the remote control to your mind. You might not want to admit it, but I will admit it for you. He has control of your mind. He has altered your joy, your peace, and your outlook on your life.

That one situation is first triggered in your **memory**. Next, your **imagination** comes on the scene and magnifies it far worse than it is. **Thoughts** are running rampant through your mind. Your **emotions** kick in and start to think for you. Your **perception** is off-balance, causing disarray in the **will** of God for your life.

Guard Your Mind

You have to break away from the world and stop being controlled by the media and by unmarried friends. Guard yourself from impoverished individuals who are always feeding you negativity. But, most of all, you have to rise above that situation that has implanted that sensor in your mind. You are more than a conqueror!

Above all else, guard your heart, guard your mind, take up the helmet of salvation, take up the mind of Christ, get a grip on your life, brush yourself off, get back in the fight, and tell the Devil, "Get out of my mind!" You have the ability to think your way out of your setbacks. Get your mind right, recapture your destiny, and be all that God created you to be.

Enough with the pity parties! Just because you lose a round doesn't mean you have to lose the fight. You're *in* the world, but not *of* the world. While the world quits, while the world is crying, you're regaining your strength, you're repositioning yourself. In the face of adversity, you're redefining yourself!

Shift!

Break away from the standards of this world and be transformed by the renewing of your mind. "How do I renew my mind?" For every negative thought, counter-attack with the Word of God. This counterattacking is vital because what the Devil says you're not, God says you are. What the Devil says you can't do, God says you can. *You can do all things through Christ that strengthens you*! (Philippians 4:13)

You will renew your mind by renewing your relationship with the Word of God. Don't just read to be reading. In whatever area you're being attacked, find the Scripture to counter attack and speak the Word of God over it. Death and life are in the power of the tongue. Declare the Word of God over your life. Believe it and receive it.

Begin to transform your thoughts, actions, and conversations according to the Word of God. I promise that you won't recognize yourself. This might be a good thing since the old you was holding you back. You will transfigure so fast that your spouse won't recognize the new you but will love the new you. Your children will smile to see you come home instead of going to hide in their rooms.

Shhhh!

By the time you put this book down, you will see life differently. Your perception is getting ready to change. Relationships will get better instead of worse. Your praise and worship will be renewed. But, most importantly, you will see yourself in a way that you never have before.

Hey, can you keep a secret? Not with me, but with yourself? The secret is that you just changed. Your mind has just been renewed. But nobody knows this except you. When you put this book down, you will be a new individual. By the time you set this book down, all possibilities will have become new!

Walk away with a smile. Embrace somebody you love, but shhhh! Don't tell them your secret. Just show them. Let that secret between you and God burn in your heart. Let that secret be the fuel to your fire. Let that secret be the secret to your success and new life in Christ Jesus. Look in the mirror and embrace the new you. You owe it to yourself.

Yield

Therefore submit to God.
Resist the devil and he will flee from you.
James 4:7

As God begins to speak to you in these pages, I have a word of advice for you: yield. Don't try to deny the facts. Don't push them to the back of your mind. Don't look to your spouse, and don't look to your neighbor. Simply yield to the voice of God.

You could've accomplished so much more if you would've simply yielded to the voice of God. When the Word of God comes forth, it's pure, rich, and cutting in every aspect. But too often you pass the blame as if the Word would've been good for the one who wasn't present, or for your neighbor, or maybe even for your spouse, who never attends. You're in denial that the Word of God is for you.

Apply the Word

Maybe your spouse will begin to accompany you to church when you begin to apply the Word of God to your life-first! You might be the reason why your spouse isn't coming. Show your spouse results by yielding to the Word of God. Allow God's Word to take root in your heart.

Lotion does you no good when you leave it on the shelf without applying it to your body. Where there is no application of lotion, the result will be an ashy body with dry skin. The same is with the word of God. You have to apply the word of God to your life in order to yield results.

Spiritually, there are too many ashy, dry Christians walking around because they aren't applying the word of God to their life. Nobody likes being ashy and nobody likes being around a dry, angry depressed Christian. Apply the word!

No Submission, No Flee

How often have you heard people say, "Resist the devil and he shall flee from you?" How true that is. But they often neglect the most important part of that verse. The first part reads, "Submit to God." People often want the devil to flee from their lives, but they are not willing to submit to the Word of God!

They are not willing to yield their will for His will. If the devil hasn't fled from your life, the first question that you must ask yourself is, "What area haven't I submitted to God?" Next, look yourself in the eye, and pose this question, "Why not?" Thirdly, answer the question! Why not? Why haven't you done what God told you to do — yet?!

What's the Problem?

Why haven't you gotten that divorce yet if you'll have been separated for five years? Why haven't you separated yourself from that one that you know is pulling you down, cheating on you, or abusing you? Why are you still drinking when you know what the doctor said?

Why are you still in leadership and openly cheating on your spouse, not willing to change or seek guidance? You have come to the altar, met with the Elders of the church, cornered the Pastor while at Wal-Mart, cried, had people listen to you, and received a corrective directional Word from the Lord. Yet you refused to yield to God's counsel—and you want the devil out of your life!

Many of you want the curse to be removed, and you want the slandering to stop, and you want to stop being hurt. I have a suggestion for you. How about yielding to God? Pay your tithes, stop fornicating, and come out of that adultery. Put the bottle down, and leave the drugs alone: yield!

Submit It

I promise you that if you submit your desires, weaknesses, and habits to God, the devil will flee from you. The devil will have to flee because he will no longer have anything to identify with inside of you.

This lack of submission explains why the devil hasn't fled from you yet. It's because you haven't submitted everything to God. Some of you haven't submitted *anything* to God. That very thing that you haven't submitted to God is what the devil is controlling you by.

You're his little puppet, and he's controlling your strings. You're his remote control car, and he has the remote. It's pathetic, and everybody sees it and knows it except you—all because you refuse to deal with yourself, and because you refuse to submit to God!

No Vacancies

This very principle of submission and identification is what made Jesus so powerful. While speaking with His disciples about the adversary, Jesus declared with boldness and authority, *"He has nothing in Me"* (John 14:30). Jesus was serving notice to every eavesdropping demon, and to Satan himself, that there was nothing inside of Him that Satan's army could latch themselves onto.

There was nothing inside of Him that they could identify with in conjunction with their sinful ways. Jesus yielded every area to the Word of God, and, in return, Satan had no control over His life.

Satan and his imps had no choice but to flee. When it came to Jesus they were wasting their time because they could find no place to stay. So they moved on to the next contestant that they could dominate because of lack of submission: you!

Amen

To get a better understanding, let's break down the word *yield*. To *yield* means to stop opposing or resisting, and to agree to somebody's demands or requests. I challenge you to stop opposing and resisting the Word of the Lord, even when you don't understand it, and even when you don't feel like it. I beseech you to agree with God's demands and requests that He has placed through His Word.

Signify that you agree by simply saying "Amen" when God speaks to you. No more "what-ifs," and no more "buts." It's time for you to get your "buts" out of the way. Your "buts" are what got you in this predicament in the first place. "Buts" never yield; they always oppose and resist. "Buts" always try to justify their sins and make the Word conducive to their lives. Do yourself a favor: Get your "but" out of the way!

This revelation is significant because God isn't through with you yet. You haven't even scratched the surface of what God has for you. This brings me to my next point. The name of this chapter is *Yield*, not *stop*. God wants you to stop *doing* you, but He doesn't want you to stop *being* you: There's a difference!

Clichés

Have you ever found yourself saying, "I'm going to keep it real," and you end up saying something degrading, only to offend someone around you? You're keeping it real alright—real stupid! You're showing your ignorance.

When someone questions you about why you act the way that you act, you simply blurt out, "Well, that's just how I am!" No, no, no, no, no! God is saying, "That might be how you are, but that's not how I am." In other words, "That might be who you are in the carnal, but that's not how I made you in the spirit."

Stop, but Don't Stop

Stop saying what you want to say, and stop doing what you want to do. It doesn't work like that with God— maybe in your world, but not in God's world. So what am I saying? Lose the godliness, but keep your personality. Lose the sin, but keep your style. Lose the profanity, but keep the humor. Lose the pride, but keep the confidence. Stop doing you, but never stop being you.

Many times when we are corrected, we shut down and withdraw altogether. We call Pity over to the party and we began to converse with ourselves. "I can't do anything right! Every time I try to do something, I always mess up. I can't satisfy anybody. Nobody appreciates me. I might as well stop trying." When you start thinking like that, you will stop in your tracks and failure will become inevitable.

This is how people are often robbed of their destiny. The adversary gets in their minds, and they become unfruitful. Rather than yielding, they stop in the middle of life with their arms folded, pouting over corrections, disciplines, and chastisements. They are only hurting themselves and their destinies.

Get Back in the Race

Do yourself a favor. Get your mind right! Unfold those arms, crank the car of hope back up, put it in drive, and proceed with your life. In the traffic world, *yield* doesn't mean *stop*. It simply means "proceed with caution."

As you approach the next intersection of life, I urge you to yield to the voice of the Lord. Go where He tells you to go. Do what He tells you to do. Say it how He tells you to say it. But don't stop. Simply proceed with caution.

Facing Your Fears

But when he saw that the wind was boisterous, he was afraid.
Matthew 14:30

I f only everyone knew the true you. Your image and your actualities are far from matching each other. I must give it to you. You're one aggressive, strong-minded, and talented individual. It's a shame that you have allowed fear to cripple you.

Fear laughs at you and mocks you in the pits of Hell: "Everybody thinks they are so powerful and so deep, but I've got them scared to death! They will never amount to anything!" If the devil and his demons never told the truth before, they just did. With fear being so evident in your life, you will never amount to anything. You will literally be scared till your death!

Fear over Faith

Fear cripples you. Fear rushes through the bloodstream, paralyzes your mind, delays your actions, and causes you to become motionless. And for the last couple of years, **you have been walking in the natural, but motionless in the spirit,** all because of fear. You have nobody to blame but yourself!

You chose fear over faith. You should be much further along by now, but you have allowed fear to invade your success. You talk a good one, preach a good one, and can write up a good vision, but the devil knows—and you know— that you really aren't anything because you're scared!

What If

Fear of failing, fear of stepping out, and fear of what others are going to think or say are just a few thoughts that have hindered your success. **Instead of thinking about what happens if you do step out, you need to think about what happens if you don't step out!** How many people will be affected if you don't do what God is calling you to do? What abundance will your family, church, and community miss because of your fears?

Fear is selfish. All it thinks about is itself. Fear only has its best interest at heart and never thinks about others. And since you have allowed fear to reside in you, you are being selfish to those who are depending on you. Stop thinking about yourself and do what God is calling you to do!

Fear and Pride

Fear is self-centered and egotistical. Your fear of failing is connected to your ego, which is connected to your pride. You have too much pride to step out of the boat for fear of getting your image tarnished or your reputation wet with the challenges that come with trusting God.

Pride comes before the fall, but you have a God who is able to keep you from falling! You have to trust God and be committed to pleasing Him even at the expense of what others might say or think about you. Forget about your image, stop trying to crunch the numbers, and just get out of the boat!

Get Out of the Boat

Peter was faced with these same challenges. You can say what you want to say about Peter, but at least he stepped out of the boat! What about the other eleven disciples? Even His most faithful, the beloved John, passed on this go-round. This lets me know that even the most beloved and the most faithful are also faced with fear.

The story reads that *The wind was contrary* (Matthew 14:24). This seems to be your situation as well. Everything seems contrary to what God is telling you to do, but that's when you know it's God speaking! In spite of how it looks now versus how it looked when you first heard God, you have to get out of the boat! You can find peace in the following words.

Be of good cheer. It is I; be not afraid. Matthew 14:17

The Lord is saying, "Be of good cheer; I'm the one that told you to start that new business. Be of good cheer;

I'm the one who told you to write that book. Be of good cheer; I'm the one who told you to apply for that job. Be of good cheer; I'm the one who told you to start that church. That voice that you heard was me, Jesus. And since I'm the one who placed it in your spirit, you don't have to be afraid!"

Come

Whatever God is requesting you to do—do it! Be not afraid. You're at a place in life where you must conquer your fears. You must do as Peter did and take that initial step. "*Come.*" The Lord didn't give Peter any long explanation or plea. When challenged if it was He, the Lord simply said, "*Come.*"

Many of you have been looking for confirmation from the Lord. You have a new venture brewing in your spirit, and you're looking for a sign from the Lord to move forward. The Lord is simply saying, "*Come.*" And since the Lord said, "*Come,*" I'm telling you to go! Peter did what you haven't done yet. He did what the others didn't have the heart to do. He took that initial step and got out of the boat.

Fear of Starting

After you conquer the fear of failing, you must conquer the fear of starting. Have you ever been in a place where you have a vision from God—clear as day—but when it gets to the point of execution of the vision, the voice of fear begins to speak?

But this time, the fear is accompanied with confusion. You get so afraid and confused in what God showed you or told you that you do what most people do, which is nothing at all! You have become paralyzed by your fears because you have a fear of starting.

Unbelievable

Just imagine climbing down a boat and taking your first step to walk on water. Peter had the naysayers behind him, the uncanny around him, and the unfamiliar under his feet. One thing he had working for him was whom he had in front of him—Jesus! With Jesus on your side, you can conquer your every fear. The Bible states that Peter, a man who did the impossible, "walked on the water."

That's exactly what you're capable of when you resolve to get out of the boat. You're capable of doing the unbelievable. You're capable of walking on your situations, and you're capable of defying gravity.

Those things that were designed to hold you back will be under your feet! You have the ability to break limits, remove restrictions, and redefine yourself when you conquer your fears. You must stay focused and keep your trust in God and not in yourself. When you get away from these principles, failure is inevitable.

Fear of Finishing

But when he saw the wind boisterous, he was afraid, and began to sink.
Matthew 14:30

The eccentric thing about these matters is this: The boisterous winds were always there, but Peter had a fear of finishing. Matthew clearly noticed and noted this in verse 24 of the chapter. But somewhere along the journey, the voice that told Peter to "come" became fuzzy. The trust in that voice weakened as his settings around him got stronger.

The contrary winds were always around him. Their impact was evident before he got out of the boat. Peter looked where he had come from, where he was, and what he was getting ready to accomplish. In return, fear set in, and he lost his focus and began to sink.

"What am I doing out here? I'm not supposed to be this far out! I'm not supposed to be walking on water. I'm not capable of this. Nobody has done this before. I'll never make it across. Everybody is going to laugh at me if I fail."

Those brief seconds probably felt like an eternity to Peter. But these were conversations that he had with himself. **Nobody verbally doubted him or told him he**

couldn't do it, but somewhere along the line, he began to doubt himself. Peter had a fear of finishing, and so do you.

No More Questions

That voice that told you to start will be there to make sure you finish. Never allow the storms of life to bring you to the question, "Did I really hear from God?" This question will pull your eyes off God and place them on your own capabilities. Fear, doubt, and disbelief are bound to set in.

You'll realize how far you are from the boat, and you will begin to ponder those same dreaded thoughts Peter pondered. "What am I doing here? I'm not capable of this. I'll never be able to pull this off." These are all symptoms that fear is on the prowl, but don't give up!

Stretch

And immediately Jesus stretched forth his hand and caught him.
Matthew 14:31

The sad thing about this story is Peter was closer to his destination than he thought. Matthew recorded that his destiny was within arm's reach. He was so close that all Jesus had to do was stretch out his hand.

You're not as far away as you think either. You're within arm's reach of your breakthrough. All you have to do is stretch out! Don't give up. Be steadfast; be unmovable. It's when you're at the point of breakthrough that the waves of life kick up to try to get you to turn back. Stay focused, and keep your eyes open. Fear is on the prowl, but I see a Savior heading your way!

Facing the Familiar

Have I been with you so long?
John 14:9

O k then; let's see what's next on the list. Ah, here we go. Let's chat about your spiritual life. Lately you have seemed kind of—what's the word I'm looking for here—*dead*. Your relationship with God seems to have gotten tedious.

You seem dull—stagnate. My question for you is: What happened to your zeal? Come on, where's your passion? When I see you, I don't see enthusiasm; I see dullness, insipidness. There's no flavor; there's no fervor in your spirit. What happened? What went wrong? What seems to be the issue? I know what the issue is: It's you!

You Changed

It has to be you because it isn't Jesus. The Bible says that *Jesus is the same yesterday, today, and forever* (Hebrews 13:8). He didn't change—you changed. Maybe you didn't change *per se*, but your perspective changed. The way you view Christ changed. The way that you receive Him changed. The way that you feel about Him changed. Why? Because *you* allowed it to change!

You alone are solely responsible for your spiritual life. You can have as much of Christ as you want. Nobody is stopping you from pursuing Christ but you. Stop blaming others for your stagnation; get up and pursue Christ!

What Happened

Often when I talk to people, they say things to me like, "I used to be like you," referring to my passion for the Lord. My question to them is, "What happened? What do you mean that you *used to*?! Did God change? Did Jesus change His mind about how He feels about you? Then why did you change your feelings about Him?"

I'm not talking about aged saints. I'm talking about those who have plenty of life in them! What happened? Where did they go wrong? They went wrong the same place where you went wrong. They got too familiar with Christ, they got too familiar with the Scriptures, and they got too familiar with themselves. I'm here to tell you that becoming too familiar will kill you, and that's exactly what happened to your passion. It's been murdered!

There are three mindsets that you must stay away from: the familiar, complacency, and routines. These three mindsets are deadly! You must be sober and be vigilant against them! If you allow yourself to fall into the "church routine," you will succumb to just going through the motions.

I didn't say if you allow the devil to get you into the "church routine"; I said if you allow yourself. Yes—he will come and suggest it, but it's up to you not to allow it! You are responsible for your actions and non-actions. Get up and get your passion back! *Seek the Lord while He may be found* (Isaiah 55:6). If you wait too long, you'll become like those that I often talk to—the "used to be" people!

The Living Word

Never get too familiar with Christ and what He has done for you! Never get too familiar with John 3:16. Never allow that passage to become so familiar to you that it loses its potency! Never read over Scriptures that you know—or you think that you know—and allow them to lose their power.

There's power in John 3:16! There's still power in Romans 10:9! There's still power in Isaiah 53:5! What about Genesis 1:26? What about Jeremiah 29:11? Good God Almighty!!! What about Psalms Chapter 23? I don't know about you, but the Lord is still my Shepherd, and I'm still not wanting! There's still power in the blood, and there's still power in that name! I feel like having some *church!*

Form of Godliness

When you get too familiar with the Scriptures, you allow them to lose power in your life. I didn't say that the Scriptures lose power; I said you allow them to lose power in your life! This is what Paul was speaking about when he mentioned those who have a form of godliness but deny its power.

I don't know about you, but I don't just want a form of godliness. I want the fullness thereof! Get away from shapes and forms of God. Get away from routines and traditions. *Stir yourself up and take hold of the Lord!* (Isaiah 64:7)

This is a must because when you get too familiar with Christ and His Scriptures, you're destined to get too familiar with yourself. It's Christ and His words that set the tone for your life. So if you become stagnate in Him, you will become stagnate in yourself. You will deny His power and His daily bread for your life.

You will come to church, but you will never become the church! You will keep coming to church with a form of godliness, with your new suit or your new hat, but ultimately you will deny the power thereof. You won't be able to receive deeper levels and greater heights because you feel as if you've heard this before.

But let me tell you something—there's more revelation to be revealed in Psalms 23 and many other "familiar passages" than you could ever imagine. Don't limit God, and don't limit yourself! Open your heart, and open your mind. There's much more to receive from the Lord.

Works, Labor, No Passion

There was a church in Ephesus that was similar to you. They had works, they had labor, and they had patience, and they couldn't tolerate those who were evil. They persevered and labored for His namesake and didn't become weary. But Christ had one thing against them; they forgot their first love (Revelations 2:1-4).

They forgot what it was all about. They got used to coming in and going out. They were doing the work of the ministry but in a routine mindset. They were lacking that love for it that they used to have. They were lacking that zeal that once sparked them. They weren't weary, but their inspiration was. Christ noticed it, and possibly so did others.

Christ has also noticed that your passion has depleted. And if Christ has noticed, so have others. Your lack of passion has deterred your witness and impact for the Kingdom of God. There are three things you must do in order not to fall into familiar, complacent routines. The word of the Lord is this: *You must remember, repent, and do!* (Revelations 2:5)

Remember, Repent, Do

You have to remember the spiritual high from which you have fallen. You have to recapture that love. Recapture that passion. Remember how you felt when you heard His voice for the first time. Remember how you felt when He first touched you, when He first healed you, and when He first delivered you!

Didn't He do it? Didn't He make a way out of no way? The same one that did it back then is the same one that's on the throne today! The same praise that you gave Him back then, He deserves today, if not greater! He took you from glory to glory. So you should take your praise from glory to glory! All God is asking you to do is remember!

When you remember how much He loves you, and when you remember how much He has done for you, He leaves you with no choice but to repent! "Lord, I repent for taking You for granted. Lord, I repent for getting too familiar with You. Lord, I repent for just going through the motions! Lord, I repent for denying Your power! Lord, I remember; Lord, I repent; Lord, I'm sorry!"

The word *repent* doesn't just mean to ask for forgiveness. *Repent* also means to change your way of thinking. God is telling you to change the way that you view Him, to change the way you view His scriptures, and to change the way that you view yourself. Change your perspective, and He'll change your life!

Once you remember and once you repent, God will place a "do it" in your spirit! He will recharge you, He will renew you, and He will refresh you to do it again! Do what again? Do the first works, but with a new anointing. Do the first works, but with a new perspective. Do whatever you were doing before you lost your passion.

God will give you grace for the race! He will give you the zeal to labor more abundantly than anyone else around you. *Yet it is not you, but His grace that is with you!* (1 Corinthians 15:10) But in order for you to get your passion back, you must face Self.

A.B. Almore

Facing Self

Afterward, his brother came out, and his hand took hold of Esau's heel.
Genesis 25:26

I want you to take a moment to step back, recap, and revisit the old you. I want you to pause. Clear your mind, get out of the routines of life, and recapture yourself. Take a minute to really think about you—the real you, and the other side of you. You know, the old you who wasn't afraid to dream. The old you refused to be stopped by any means.

Think about the old you who had visions when there was no provision, and the you that, against all odds, had a mind to achieve significant greatness. What happened to that part of you? You had hope, you had inspiration, and you had tenacity. You had plans, you had goals, and you had confidence towards life until _____ happened. You fill in the blank.

Shattered Dreams

Instead of dreams, you have fears. Instead of passion, there's apathy. Instead of vision, there's complacency. Instead of greatness, there's stagnation. You have become stuck! Hope has been replaced with despair, inspiration has been substituted with jadedness, and tenacity has been swapped with double-mindedness.

Somewhere in the transition from dreams to reality, you have lost your focus. You have lost your passion for life. You have derailed your plans. Now you're just going through the motions, going with the flow, quiet, trying not to offend anybody. You are afraid of what people might say and what they may think if you release the real you. You had plans, you had goals, and you had confidence towards life until Self showed up!

Self

Self got in the way. Self shut you down. Self sat you down, and Self crippled you! You want to know why? Because Self was afraid of losing you to success. So in return, Self became that wicked twin, that unwanted roommate, and that lazy, shiftless, and stubborn egocentric side of you.

Self didn't want to let you go for fear that things would change. Self was too afraid of responsibility, too afraid of commitment, and too afraid of losing you to success. He was afraid of losing the good old days of sitting on the couch doing zilch, and the good old days of lying around in bed half the day accomplishing absolutely nothing!

Now, you can see it, but you can't become it. You can dream it, but you can't release it. You can hear it, but you can't achieve it. Something is holding you back, something is holding you down, and something won't let you go. It's that other side of you—your opposing twin named Self.

The Evil Twin

Who is Self and what's its motive? It's that lazy, complacent, and slothful side of you. It knows that it can't go with you onto the next level, but it doesn't want to lose you. In return, you compromise with it by living a double-minded, double-standard life.

One day you're an achiever; the next day you're a slacker. One day you're focused; the next day you're aimless. Don't you know that a double-minded individual shall receive nothing from the Lord? (James 1:7-8)

How can one be double-minded unless there are two minds in him or her? There are two agendas working in you; there are two separate motives. There's a war going on inside you similar to the one inside Rebekah when she was pregnant with Jacob and Esau. *The children struggled together within her* (Genesis 25:22).

Paul was also familiar with this war. He writes, *"But I see another law in my members, warring against the law of my mind, and bringing me into captivity"* (Romans 7:23). You should be able to identify with these scenarios just by looking at these passages. One passage describes it as a struggle while the other passage describes it as a war!

Held Back

There was a struggle going on inside Rebekah, and there's a struggle going on inside you. There was a war going on inside Paul, and there's a war going on inside you. Paul had two agendas inside him, pulling him on both sides, with his soul stuck in the middle. The frustration comes when you can see it but can't seem to do anything about it. You are falling captive to the weaker you spiritually, but to the stronger you carnally.

Have you ever been in a place where you tried to move forward, but something was holding you back? This is what Jacob was doing to Esau. Esau had burst through to his new beginning, but his twin brother was holding him back. His twin brother had a grip on his heel and didn't want Esau to receive what was rightfully his.

How many times has your spirit burst through the heavens, received a fresh word from God, equipped with instructions, but the fearful, idle side of you won't let you go? It just keeps holding you back. That other side of you doesn't want you to receive what's rightfully yours.

In reality it doesn't mind the success, but it quivers at the commitment. It trembles at the work, effort, and commitment that it's going to take to become successful.

In return, it tells you to chill. It persuades you that this level is ok. It says, "Hey, your bills are paid, you're living paycheck to paycheck, but who cares? You might not be positively affecting lives, but let somebody else do that."

Look Within

Your twin is talking you right out of your fate. The voices from the outside are not holding you back; the voices from the inside are. As a result, you compromise, you settle, and you abort your destiny. But if you don't understand that the hindrance is coming from the inside, you will continuously look outside for the issue.

Self will continue to fly under the radar, happy as can be. In every area across the board mentally, spiritually, and emotionally, you will become like a yo-yo: a double-minded yo-yo. You will be up one day and down the next because deep down inside, you know that there's much more, but you can't seem to grasp that it's Self that's holding you back.

For years you've channeled your energy and troubleshooting efforts into the wrong places. It's time for you to examine Self and break free from the greatest stronghold in your life—you! How do you break free?

Others

In order to break free from Self, you have to understand Self. Self is so hard to deal with because Self hides behind three wiles from the inside. Self waits on others, Self depends on others, and Self blames others. If Self can successfully plot these schemes, it will always take the spotlight off "I" and place the blame on "You."

You will never assume responsibility for your actions or for your lack of actions. It will always be someone else's fault. You will waste your life looking for handouts while waiting on others and depending on others. You will never "man up" because you're constantly blaming others. If you never get to the root of the issue, you will live a defeated life, full of excuses.

Stop waiting on others; get up and do it yourself! It's not your spouse or your job holding you back. It's you! Stop depending on others for your breakthrough. God gave you gifts and talents, and God gave you His Spirit. Shake yourself from that pity party, get back in the fight, and become everything that God is calling you to be!

Bye-Bye, Self

Self no longer has a voice. Self has no say-so. Self has no options. From here on out, nobody is asking for Self's input! Feel the opposite of what Self feels! Say the opposite of what Self says! Do the opposite of what Self does! Silence your flesh, starve your fears, and embrace your future! And whether Self likes it or not, get ready to face that weight!

A.B. Almore

Disclaimer Notice: This chapter isn't meant to be rude or viewed as a joke. This chapter is meant to save lives. Please read it all the way through.

Facing Your Weight

Whose God is their belly?
Philippians 3:19

O k; this is what I want you to do. I want you to get somewhere alone in a spacious place where there's a mirror. Next, I want you to unclothe yourself and take a slow 360-degree turn, never taking your eyes off the mirror. Lastly, I want you to deal with yourself really well.

Take heed to those stretch marks, embrace those love handles, and take special notice of that stomach. My God! What in the world do you have going on with that body? You're a little on the heavy side. No, that's not good enough. Listen to me very carefully; you are fat! There! Are you happy?

The Truth

You've been waiting for somebody to tell you that so that you could get yourself together. You've been waiting for somebody to be real with you. You've been waiting for somebody to check you and put you in place! Other people have tried to give you hints, be nice about it, or overlook it, but let me bring it to your face! You need to face your weight.

You're stout; you're obese. It's not cute, and it's not funny. It's ridiculous! Every other pep talk hasn't worked. Every other book and diet has failed and left you looking like this! I have a one-step diet for you. It's called "Deal with yourself." This is absurd! Go ahead, you can cry about it, you can pout about it, and you can email me about it, but when the smoke clears, what are you going to *do* about it?!

Until now, you haven't done anything about it except put pounds on top of pounds! You know that what I'm saying is true! It's time to deal with yourself. I don't care who else is overweight. Your pounds are *your* pounds, and their pounds are *their* pounds. Stop conforming to other people's obesity to make yourself feel better. And please stop blaming others that cook well for your eating habits.

And by no means is this chapter speaking to those who have legitimate health issues who can't lose weight or who may be facing other challenges that contribute to their size. This chapter is speaking to those who are practicing lack of self control by choice and participating in a glutton lifestyle by preference. Something has to change!

Powerless

Just because they cook does not mean that you have to eat. Are they holding you hostage and forcing you to eat? I didn't think so. The only thing holding you hostage is your flesh. But how is that with your Holy-Ghost-filled, fire-baptized self?

How are you that anointed and have no control over your own spirit? How are you that anointed and you can't control what you eat? Don't you know that *he that has no rule over his own spirit is like a city that is broken down without walls?* (Proverbs 25:28) I'm tired of seeing broken-down Christians leading the statistics in many health issues due to poor eating habits!

What type of example are you modeling for people if you're overweight? What type of spirit-led life are you representing? I'm talking to everyone, including the Deacons, Ministers, Elders, Pastors, Overseers, Bishops, and those holding authority in the Body of Christ.

Your belly is an outward display of lack of discipline and self-control. We want people to follow us, but what are they following? What do we have that they

don't have? Oh I get it, we have power in every area—
except over the food we eat!

The Stakes Are High

Is there no balm in Gilead? Is there no physician
there? Does the one who delivers not care about your
weight? Is God not mighty in this area as well? He is! The
same God that helped you stop cursing, drinking, and
lying is the same God that will strengthen you to lose that
weight!

That is, if you desire to see the results of your
ministry; if you desire to see and enjoy your grandchildren
growing up. You are called and anointed for ministry,
right? Then God has work for you to do. All that weight is
going to slow you down and deplete your energy. It could
very well shorten your lifespan.

If you're anointed now, how much greater would
you be if you were lighter on your feet and had blood
flowing more freely through your veins? Now that's next
level living. Not a new house, not a new car, or a new suit
or dress. But you losing that weight is next level!

Stop Compromising

By no means am I using my freedom of speech to bash leadership. But we **all** have to come to a place where we understand that nobody is exempt from this. From the front to the back, we're **all** in this together. This was a tough chapter to write, but going to people's funerals before their time is tougher. That's what fueled this chapter.

God doesn't want to see His people leave this earth before their time all for the love of grease and sugars! The majority of the diseases that people face today are tied directly to their eating habits. Understand this: **Death and life are in the power of the tongue: your taste buds!**

Don't eat yourself to an early grave, leaving your family, friends, and ministries behind! It's not worth your loved ones being left behind because you couldn't put the sweets down. It's not worth an early checkout because of fatty foods. The alcohol and cigarettes aren't worth it either! Do it for your family, do it for your friends, and do it for yourself!

You Can Do It!

Your family and your friends are all fine and dandy, but do it for yourself. You owe it to yourself.

Imagine a better you: feeling better, looking better, and breathing better. Who says it's too late to start? Start now, start today, and start slow. Maybe you can't start off running, so start off walking. You didn't put it all on in one day, and you won't be able to take it all off in one day.

Don't set super-high goals that you know you can't achieve. That will only cost you to get frustrated, doubt the entire process, and abort the mission. Start small so you can celebrate progress. Today's victories will give you momentum for tomorrow. A journey of a thousand miles starts with one step. So get up, brush yourself off, and take that first step today!

It's time to face your weight. There is no more looking in the mirror without looking at yourself. Take a good look at those grooves, and take a good look at those ripples and dents. Take a deep breath and say, "This is going to be the last time I see myself looking like this." Mean it this time!

Practical Approach

Often, the food or the sweets aren't the problem. The problem is the portions that we consume. There's nothing wrong with having a cookie or two. But it's a problem when you eat the entire bag in one sitting. I challenge you to work on your portions. If you're still hungry after the meal and dessert, try snacking on an apple, pear, or orange—something that holds more nutritional value than another piece of fried chicken.

If you're not overweight, or if you're young, that still doesn't give you the right to overindulge. You want have that metabolism forever and it will be sure to catch up with you in the long run. If you can't afford a gym membership, try walking around your neighborhood or your mall.

You will find this to be cost-effective while still yielding the same results. I guarantee you that if you cut all those fast foods out, you'll be able to save for a gym membership. I challenge you to go on a 30-day fast from fast foods. You'll be amazed at the increase in finances and the decrease in weight. What do you have to lose except a few pounds?

A.B. Almore

Facing the Numbers

In the house of the wise are stores of choice food and oil, but a
<u>foolish man</u> devours all he has.
Proverbs 21:20

Alrighty. Next on the list, let's deal with those finances. Ok then…wow! (Clueless look here) How can I put this? Ah, there we go. You're broke! You're living paycheck to paycheck! I mean come on…this is ridiculous!

Based on your W2's over the last couple of years, it seems that God has done His part, but you have done a pitiful job doing yours. He has blessed you, but you haven't been a good steward of the blessings.

You talked about saving this, you talked about saving that. You're just a bunch of talk and everybody knows it, including your spouse. That's why they ignore you when you get into those "saving money frenzies."

They know you never keep your word. The frenzies last all of two seconds, and you find yourself back at square one, if not worse. You're looking for answers and for someone to blame. There you go again, blaming your spouse! It's not your spouse; it's you! You are the problem!

Where Is It

You are the financial demon that's been robbing your family. You have no self-control. I dare you to pull out your W2's and your savings and checking account information and face the numbers. What do you have to show for it? Oh, a brand new dress? I'm sorry; I didn't see that over there.

What else do you have? Twenty pairs of shoes? My fault; they look so much like the rest—I must have overlooked them. You have a big-screen TV? That's a nice TV! But how is that going to help put your children through college?

I like that overpriced dining room set! But the only problem is that it is overpriced. And since you're so ignorant and impatient, you financed it at almost a 30 percent interest rate! Oh, I'm sorry; I meant 22—like that's any better!

And it's a shame—you only purchased those things to impress other people. Can I tell you a little secret? Those people don't care! They may come by and enjoy it, sit in it, and eat on it, but when they leave, you are stuck with the bill!

Stop Showing Off

Financially, you are a fool! You look like you have it together, but that look—and trying to impress other people—is what got you in trouble. You're not all that! You are a fool that has no self-control over money! Money controls you; you don't control it.

No wonder you have become stagnate in life financially. If God can't trust you with what you have, how can He release more? The Scripture is clear: *A foolish man spendeth it up* (Proverbs 21:20). You're spending everything that you're getting!

It's time for you to humble yourself! Get that pride out of your life and bring some self-control in! It's time for you to wake up, come out of that fantasy land, and face the numbers.

Face It

When is the last time you actually opened your bank statement and analyzed your spending habits? I can tell what your priorities are by where you spend your money. I can tell where you're heading by where you've been financially. Many of you don't open your statements because of fear—fear of facing the reality that you're broke and in the negative!

You don't want to face how much you spend eating out each month. Three-quarters of your income has been spent on eating out and other poor habits. You are being wasteful with your finances, and your blessings are literally *wasting* away! It's a little disgusting, but truthful.

Besides, the way you have been wasting money is disgusting.

Over the last five years, you have brought in some serious cash, but you have nothing to show for it. The opening Scripture speaks of a wise man that has treasures, choices, and oil in his household. There is no lack; there is no shortage. There is only overflow—choices of what to eat, what to wear, and what to drive, and enduring riches, all because *he possesses wisdom to handle the blessings*.

Get Some Self-Control

You're enjoying choice foods and a wide closet selection, but you're in debt! It's all on your credit cards and tied up in loans. There is no overflow, except the overflow of bills, the overflow of stress, and the overflow of lack! It's all because you don't want to make a couple of changes, deny a couple of pleasures, and practice a little self-control. I want you to hear me clearly: You did this! You were too busy living for the moment and never for the future.

That dress didn't purchase you; you purchased it. You got in your car, you drove to the mall, you got out of your car, walked right into the store, picked out that dress, tried it on, turned around in the mirror, smiled to yourself, took it to the register, applied for the charge card, got your extra 15% off, grabbed that bag, walked out of the store, and completely ignored the Holy Spirit. The entire time,

He was telling you to put that back; you don't need that; you can't afford that!

Maybe it was that car you wanted, or maybe that suit. Whatever the case may be, the scenario was the same, and the results were the same. You couldn't afford it, and the Holy Spirit told you that, but you ignored Him. You chose temporary happiness and long-term grief.

When you were trying on that dress or that fresh new suit or test-driving that new car, the internal conversation was the same. "Oh, wait till they see me in this! I'm going to be killing them!" Truth be told, you're only killing yourself. You have too much pride and arrogance to be rich. People will see you more than they will see God!

Stop Eating Your Seeds

Stop wearing your seeds on your back! Stop driving in your seeds to impress others! Get your insecure self somewhere and sit down! Clothes and things don't make you. It's God that should bring forth that fulfillment.

Stop wasting your seeds and stop eating your seeds. The only reason why you eat the way you eat is because of the temporary comfort that it brings. You wouldn't be so stressed out if you were being a better steward of your finances.

Comfort foods are not the answer! They are depleting your funds. You always enjoy eating out until the bill comes because you know better. You know what I'm saying is true. It's time to face the numbers.

Stop wasting your blessings! I want to introduce you to three words you might not be familiar with. They are: *save, save,* and *save!* When you want to go out to eat or to the mall, counteract by saving that money instead.

But I'm not saying that you can't enjoy life or that you should hoard everything you have. I encourage you to go on trips, and I encourage you to go on vacations. But I also encourage you to plan for them. You have to get away from impulsive outings and purchases.

Plan, Budget, Save

When going to the grocery store, plan a list and a budget, and take only that amount with you. If you run over what's in your wallet, put something back—no more impulsive buying while walking down the aisles. You don't need it. You saw it, and it created a need for itself. If you didn't plan for it, then don't get it!

I would like to encourage you to plan for your future. I know you would like to think that you're going to be 40 going on 19 forever, but that's not reality. You have to face the numbers of age and retirement funds. I know God will take care of your needs according to His riches and glory, but He wants to do this through your retirement funds.

Shake that fear of not understanding the benefits of it, and shake that fear of getting old. Stop procrastinating! Find somebody to educate you on your finances, your retirement funds, and your saving needs.

Your bank will be a good place to start if you have an account. If you don't have an account, go get one today and ask about the bank's financial programs. The bank will be more than glad to assist you when you're ready to assist yourself. So do yourself a favor and go ahead and face the numbers.

A.B. Almore

Why Face the Num|

*And **you** shall know the truth, and the truth shall set **you** jì.*
John 8:32

Why face the numbers, you might ask? The Scripture above answers it perfectly. "***You*** shall know the truth and the truth shall set ***you*** free." ***You*** will never be free financially unless ***you*** know where ***you're*** at!

I would like to point out that the Scripture says that ***you*** should know the truth and not your neighbor. ***You*** have to lay everything out before ***you*** in order to get a clear snapshot of where ***you're*** at. I'm talking doctor bills, past-due bills, student loans—the whole shebang.

Enough Is Enough

You must realize that ***you*** aren't bringing God any glory with debt collectors calling ***your*** house. ***You're*** not bringing God any glory with insufficient funds in ***your*** account. How is that representing the King? Is that showing that He's all-powerful and that He takes care of His children? No, it doesn't. He is all-powerful, and He does take care of His children, but ***you*** have to take better care of ***your*** finances.

Certain things and certain terminology shouldn't exist in your vocabulary. Let me run through them for you: Past due, Insufficient Funds, Derogatory Credit, Negative Balances, Overdrawn, Over Limit, Declined, Late Fees, Payment Arrangements, Paycheck-to-Paycheck, Return Checks, Post-Dated Checks—and the list goes on.

Change Your Thinking

Show me in the Bible where the people of God should be living like this. You must break free from these strongholds and begin declaring the Word of God over your life!

You need to wake up, smell the coffee, stop making excuses, stop settling for less, and claim your inheritance! Stop accepting what life is bringing to you, and start accepting the Word of God. You are God's child! Stop living beneath your means!

You are above and not beneath. You are the head and not the tail! You shall lend and not borrow! You shall owe no man anything but love! Everything that your hand touches is blessed! You are blessed coming in, and you are blessed coming out! You are favored by God. You're more than a conqueror, and you will conquer this debt!

It's time to come back to your senses! You are a child of the King! The hired servants in the Kingdom have food enough to spare, and here you are in life starving?

The devil is a liar!!! You are a child of God, the seed of Abraham. Claim what's rightfully yours, and manage it right this time!

Position Yourself

God wants to bless your socks off! God wants to pour out such a blessing that there want be enough room to receive it! But you have to be able to handle it. You will never be able to handle it tomorrow if you don't face the numbers today. Don't wait until you get this big check to start saving. Start today!

Go to the bank and deposit five dollars in your savings today. Mentally start making the changes that need to be made right now! Breakthrough isn't necessarily *when* the manifestation comes. Breakthrough is the revelation quickening in your spirit of who God is and what He's able to do. Breakthrough is you seeing the change before the change happens! Breakthrough is you seeing it, tasting it, and knowing it's there before it happens!

Redefine Yourself

You have to reach inside yourself and pull out that other you. I'm talking about the you that you see when you close your eyes. You must reach inside yourself and pull out that wealthy you. Reach inside yourself and pull out that disciplined you.

Why Face the Numbers?

There is a you that the world hasn't seen. I'm talking about that successful you and that prosperous you— dressing nice, living nice, being a blessing to others, sending others on mission trips, and fronting the bill. There is a side of you that the world hasn't seen! You must pull that side of you out, present it to the world, and bring God some glory!

I dare you to tap in. I dare you to begin to live out of the overflow and abundance of God! He has given you an inheritance that you must not squander on riotous living. Don't wait; start right now! Right where you are, make up your mind that you're going to do better, that you want better, and that better is on the way!

Face the numbers! Face the facts, face your mistakes, face your shortcomings, and face your financial failures! Repent before the Lord for being a poor steward. God will restore you. He will redeem you. He will renew you. But most importantly, He will entrust you again. But it all starts with facing the numbers. And what better time to face them than NOW!

Pride

Pride and arrogance I hate.
Proverbs 8:13

Whoa! Wait a minute. Don't be so quick to skip over this chapter—that is, if you don't have too much pride to read it! I know you feel that this chapter doesn't pertain to you, but I beg to differ. Pride is crafty, and it's devious. It knows how to camouflage itself. It could very well be there and you don't know it.

It's silent, but it speaks volumes. It's dangerous and it's destructive. It may be harboring in your heart. Take heed to this chapter, be still, and examine yourself. You are not exempt from this iniquity. As a matter of fact, I have some questions for you.

Why?

Why are you so puffed up? Why are you so conceited? Why do you feel that you're all that? Why are you so boastful? Why are you such a braggart? What makes you better than others?

Who are you? Did you create yourself? Did you bless yourself? What gives you the right to carry yourself the way that you do? You're living off borrowed wisdom and borrowed knowledge. You wouldn't have what you have if God didn't give it to you.

It's His words, it's His money, it's His world, it's His body, it's His beauty, it's His gifts, it's His talents, it's His time, it's His grace, and it's His mercy! You are nothing! Humble yourself! I suggest that you demote that pride before God demotes you!

He Hates It

God hates pride! Did you hear what I just said? God hates pride! You need to humble yourself. Tone it down! Not only does God hate pride, but He hates a prideful look (Proverbs 6:17). Just the appearance of pride is an abomination to the Lord.

Your cockiness is pushing others away from God. Pride has the ability to block out the truth. Don't allow pride to tune out what I'm saying, and please don't allow pride to isolate you from the truth.

Pride's Tactics

Pride desires to isolate you from three things: corrections, rebukes, and chastisements. Pride wants you to think that you have it all together when you really don't.

Did you know that pride keeps secrets? It doesn't keep secrets from others, but it keeps secrets from you. Everybody can see it and everybody knows it's there — except you!

Pride has been lying to you for a long time. Others tried to tell you, but you couldn't see it. Pride had you believing that you were something that you weren't. And since it isolated you from corrections, it also hindered you from changing. There was no need to change if there wasn't anything to correct.

This explains why you're at a standstill in life. You keep revisiting the same issues because they were never confronted in the first place. They were blown over, pushed under the rug, and thrown to the back of your mind because you "had it all together!"

Self-Sufficient = Insufficient

All this time, you never came to grips with Self, that you needed help. You never took the time to evaluate your life. For years, you have passed up opportunities for improvement by making excuses for yourself. Pride never admits that it's wrong or that it messed up. Pride simply covers up and keeps going through life as it is!

I know what you're thinking. "I ain't got no pride in me." Understand this—pride is silent, but it speaks. You might not know it's there, but your actions are articulating, "I don't need God!"

Pride is self-sufficient. This is one of the main reasons why God hates pride because pride keeps you away from the source—Him. God's desire is to provide for His children. In return, He seeks praise and worship.

But when people become independent and begin moving in their own strength, God is robbed of His worship. They feel no need to worship since they "made it" on their own. They don't understand that they're not sufficient to think anything on their own, but their sufficiency is from God! (2 Corinthians 3:5)

Examine Yourself

When God sees pride, He doesn't see His image; He sees Satan's image. This is why God hates a prideful look. Satan's heart was full of pride. It was his prideful heart that got him kicked out of Heaven. Satan was the first partaker in pride going before the fall! (Proverbs 16:18)

This is why it's so critical that you grasp this concept. Pride will demote you from the presence of God, and *apart from Him you can do nothing* (John 15:5). Don't allow pride to hinder your success, and don't allow pride to deter your elevation.

Be careful that you're not humble on the outside but prideful on the inside. Pride is cunning. It knows how to look and sound. Stop passing judgment on others to keep the light off you.

Pride never accepts the blame, but it's quick to pass the blame. How is it that you're never wrong and always right? Stop being blind to the fact that your mind is lopsided, negative, and forceful. Rid yourself of excuses and stop dancing around the real issue—you.

Humble Yourself

Pride is conniving. It will have you looking everywhere but on the inside for solutions. *Never have too much pride to admit that you're wrong. Never have too much pride to accept corrections or instructions. Never have too much pride to say that you don't know.*

God gives more grace to the humble, but He resists the proud. Look to God for help and acknowledge Him in all of your ways. I promise you, success is right around the corner. So my advice to you is simple. Humble yourself.

Final Thoughts

Dethroning Pride

You can dethrone pride by simply monitoring your thoughts, agenda, and motives. Examine yourself with questions such as: why am I doing this, do I just want to be seen, am I trying to make myself look good, do people see me more than they see God, is God being glorified, did God tell me to do this or is this something I want to do, am I caught up in my looks, do I think that I'm all that, am I stuck up, am I self-sufficient, do I acknowledge God in all my ways, and am I drawing people closer to me or to God? I think you get the point!

Yes You Are!

Being confident
Philippians 1:6

Allow me to let you in on a little secret that you might not know about yourself. You are insecure! I know what you're thinking. You're thinking, "No, I'm not!" But I'm here to tell you that you are!

Can I take it a step further? Your insecurities are making a fool out of you. There you go again, saying to yourself, "No, they're not." Well, I'm here to tell you that they are! How are they making a fool of you?

Effects

Your insecurities are causing you to withdraw and overreact, and to find fault in others. First result: loneliness. Second result: foolishness. Third result: ignorance! Nobody wants to be your friend because of your temper, everybody hates talking to you because you overanalyze things, and nobody likes to correct you or give you advice because you might take it the wrong way and blow up!

This psychological approach isn't doing anything but taking the heat off the real issue – you! I have some advice for you. Stop it! Deal with your insecurities.

It's a dangerous thing to be insecure and not know it. Insecurity is a silent killer, a treacherous thief, and a master of disguise. It can only be detected by honest self-examination. It camps out in your mind and takes a seat in your perceptions, causing you to view others as enemies, antagonists, and foes.

Perception = Reception

However you perceive a thing determines how you receive a thing. If you perceive me wrong, you will receive me wrong. Your insecurities are causing you to receive others wrong. Believe it or not, everybody isn't against you, and everybody isn't out to get you. Everyone isn't picking on you. Everybody isn't looking down on you, and everyone isn't talking about you behind your back. Those are your insecurities and perceptions talking to you!

Confront It

Why are you so nervous? Why are you so shy? Why are you afraid to read? Why are you afraid to talk? Why are you afraid to look others in the eye? You are insecure! "No, I'm not!" You are! Admit it, deal with it, and obliterate it!

On the flip side, why are you so prideful? Why are you so loud and offensive? What are you hiding behind all that aggressiveness? Does profanity make up for your weaknesses? Get somewhere and sit your loud mouth down! That's a cover-up to what's really going on. You're weak, you're afraid, and you're confused!

You're not as smart as they think, are you? You don't have it going on like they think you do, do you? So you cover it up with your demeanor, attitude, and arrogance. Truth be told, you're just as insecure as the timid one. Aggressive insecurity is no different from passive insecurity. Stop trying to make up for what you aren't. You look and sound foolish! Receive it, believe it, and slay that insecurity before it slays you!

You're Missing It

Your insecurities are playing mind games with you! They're robbing you of life, relationships, joy, and peace. You're missing moments and laughter all because you're too worried what somebody might be saying or thinking about you.

NEWS FLASH: They're not talking about you! They're not even thinking about you! They're out there having a blast at life while you're sitting at home miserable, pondering empty thoughts. Stop it! You're becoming bitter and negative for nothing. Nobody likes being around a bitter, negative person. But you can't see that you're the issue, so you blame others. You put up a wall, have a woe-is-me party, and isolate yourself. Satan capitalizes off the foot hold that you gave him! Now you think everyone is against you when that's simply not the case.

Stop Worrying about Them

Insecurity isn't God's will for your life. Insecurity is defined as being anxious and unstable, not being firm or steady, and lacking self-confidence. Philippians 4:6 reminds us to be *anxious for nothing. Anxious* means being worried or afraid about something that <u>might happen</u>.

You need to stop worrying and being afraid of what others <u>might be</u> thinking or saying about you. The key word in the previous two sentences is <u>*might*</u>. Nine times out of ten, what you're worrying about never happens, and nine times out of ten, people aren't saying or thinking what you think they are.

If they are, who cares? As long as you know who you are, as long as you know that you didn't say it, as long as you know that you didn't do it, who cares? It's OK to state your case. It's ok to present your side of the story. But after that, don't get consumed with it, and don't let it occupy your mind.

Those ideas and thoughts will continue to fester, overtake your life, and shift your perception in a heartbeat. They will cause you to view life through the wrong lenses. You will miss what God says about you in the following passage. *Being confident of this very thing—that he which hath begun a good work in you will perform it* (Philippians 1:6).

You're a Good Work

I'm going to allow these words from Paul to close this chapter. From this day forward, I want you to shake those lies and fears and denounce all insecurities. I want you to become confident—not cocky, but confident. Be confident of one thing—that He began a good work. He began a good work when He created you, so stop thinking that you're a bad work!

From this day forward, I want you to confess, "I'm a good work!" I didn't say it; God said it. I didn't think it; God thought it about you. If God said it and if God thought it, that's all that matters. If you weren't good, you became good when God said it! It's time for you to free yourself from labels, opinions, and past failures. God said that you are a good work—end of story!

It's in You

Where did God begin the good work? God began the good work in you! So if God began a good work in you, you have to get all that bad stuff out of you. You have to get all those negative thoughts, perceptions, recordings, and setbacks out of your life.

God has begun a good work in you, and those negative works are trying to stop what He started. But I declare in the name of Jesus that you are totally delivered from all insecurities, fears, failures, and past setbacks. Who the Son has set free is free indeed.

He's Able

And He who has begun a good work in you, will He not perform it? Will He not clean you up; will He not change your heart and your mind? Will He not heal your wounds? Will He not deliver security to the insecure?

Be confident that He will, that He can, and that He's able! Just sit back and watch God perform it. But when you sit back, do yourself a favor. Use God's lenses instead of yours. You'll be amazed at how beautiful the world and those around you really are!

Yes You Are!

Signs of Insecurity

Overanalyzing things
Holding on to comments
Feeling as if everyone is against you
Being uptight
Being skeptical
Making false assumptions
Being tense
Being angry
Being self-conscious
Trying to impress people
Being unstable
Being depressed
Overcompensating for weaknesses
Being loud (to intimidate)
Being wounded
Being timid
Being easily offended
Having low self-esteem
Always seeking the approval of others

A.B. Almore

It's Him, but It's You

For the accuser of our brethren has been cast down
Revelations 12:10

The scripture above equates to the majority of your issues. You are allowing yourself to be played by the enemy. Nobody likes to be played for a fool, and that's exactly what he's been doing to you. He has gotten into your head and whispered things about others in your ear and you fed into it!

He has played you time after time and dropped thoughts into your mind. You took them and ran with them. It's him, but it's you, too. The only power that the devil has is the power that you give him. And lately you have been giving him a lot!

Suggestions and Accusations

The devil's power rests solely in suggestions. He can't make you do or say anything. He can make the suggestion to you, but it's up to you to act on it. Throughout the Scripture, the enemy is referred to as the accuser of the brethren. The Bible says, *"He accuses us before God day and night"* (Revelation 12:10).

If the devil has the audacity to accuse us before God day and night, certainly he will make accusations about your spouse and significant others to you!

The difference between you and God is that God has enough discernment to know that it's the enemy talking—but you don't! And if you do have enough discernment, you have too much pride to shut up! You feel as if you have to get your point across. The accuser of the brethren is wreaking havoc in your life. Don't get mad at him though; get mad at yourself for letting him in!

The Plot

All day and all night, the enemy is constantly feeding negative thoughts into your mind about others. He'll accuse your spouse, he'll accuse your Pastor, he'll accuse your boss, and he'll accuse your parents—anybody that's of any value to you.

These accusations cause your emotions to burn, and your imagination begins to run wild: "I wish they would say something to me when I get home! Let that joker say one smart thing to me today!!!" Now you're upset before anything even takes place.

The accuser plants the seed and *you allow it* to grow in your mind. Did you catch that? I said you allow it to grow in your mind! Your thoughts, perception, emotions, imagination, and memory all kick in.

Your memory works against you because something similar may have happened before, so now your imagination creates a scenario that doesn't exist. Your emotions flare up and you have a perception of the individual or the event before it even takes place (*if* it takes place). All the while, the accuser of the brethren is sitting back laughing. He played you again!

The Scheme

Now he goes and visits the other individual that you're ready to clash with. He accuses you of something and gets them all rowdy, and now you have two heated individuals heading on a collision course. This is often the case for many spouses. They're each being visited by the accuser of the brethren, and all day long they are meditating on negative thoughts.

They're driving home ticked off at the other individual, thinking about what might be said, the condition of the house, and the possibility of dinner not being cooked.

On the other side, you have one that has been accused of being "used" and "overlooked" by the other, so, today, they aren't cleaning or cooking anything, and nobody had better say anything to them about it!

The devil and his imps have planted the seeds. They step out of the picture, watch both spouses arrive, and take a seat outside the living room window, slapping each other high-fives and laughing as you quarrel. You fed into the lies!

Voices

The devil is classified as the father of lies, but Jesus is classified as the Father of truth! All day long, voices and conversations are going on in your mind. Some are positive, but most are negative.

Why are most so negative? Most are negative because you're not spiritual. You relate to the carnal better than the spiritual. Therefore you give your ear to the negative—which is coming from the accuser—because you're familiar with that. But Jesus said, *"My sheep know my voice and the voice of a stranger they will not follow"* (John 10:4-5).

You have to journey deeper in the Word of God so that you can know his voice. Then when the thoughts come and they don't line up with the Word, you can say, "That's not God. God wouldn't tell me to say that." God will never tell you to curse your spouse or children. God will never tell you to cheat on your spouse.

Do It God's Way

God will never give you a license to speak your mind or let that person have it just this one time! That's not God. That's the accuser of the brethren feeding you his agenda, and you keep receiving it!

Get out of the flesh and get into the Word of God. When you get into the Word of God, you will understand that you don't wrestle against flesh and blood. You will understand that people are not your problem.

When you become more spiritual—not prideful—you will take your stance in the spirit realm instead of the natural realm. The weapons of our warfare are not carnal but mighty through God.

You will begin to realize that when you're in the flesh, you are defenseless because our weapons aren't activated by carnality. You are only mighty when you're doing it God's way and responding how He responds.

How did God respond to the accuser? He cast the accuser of the brethren down! God didn't feed into those lies; God didn't feed into all that garbage. Instead, He cast the devil down! So if God cast him down, you have no choice but to cast him down.

Cast Him Down

Stop feeding into all that garbage. Rid yourself of all that negativity. Cast him down! Get him out of your marriage! Get him out of your house! Get him out of your mind! Cast him out of your church!

Only then will you experience the fullness of life through salvation, strength, and Kingdom—living that God promised. You couldn't experience any of this before because the accuser was always nagging in your ear.

When you cast him down, take a second look at your life; go back and revisit some relationships. Cast him down and take a second look at your spouse; look again at your children. Cast him down and take a second look at your ministry. I guarantee you it's not as bad as he made it seem. So what are you waiting for? Cast him down!!!

Two-Way Street

Submitting yourselves one to another
(Ephesians 5:21)

Alrighty, let's move right along. Pull up a chair and have a seat. You look like you could use some "R&R." I'm not talking about rest; I'm talking about a little relationship reality. Whoa. Wait a minute. Don't be so quick to go to the next chapter. Trust me; this is much needed.

I'm going to let you in on a little secret. You are singlehandedly ruining your relationship. Not your spouse, not your significant other—it's you! Humble yourself, excuse pride out of this reading, and examine yourself, for what it's worth. You'll be surprised.

Trust Me

I know you think that you can go through your relationship with your eyes closed, but I'm here to open them. I know it's been 10 years, 20 years, maybe 30—but these next 15 minutes are catered just for you so that you can make it another 10, 20, or 30 years.

You have been making a mess of things, and this has been going on for a while. Problems keep growing and festering. Trust me: your spouse wanted to tell you, but he or she knew you wouldn't listen. You're too stuck in "your ways." Did you hear that? You're too stuck in *your ways*—not your spouse's. That's not what relationships are all about.

Narrow Roads

You have to come to realize that relationships are a two-way street. Growing up, I remember that any time my father was driving on a two- way street, he would always pay close attention. He understood that one false move could produce a head-on collision and cause some serious damage.

The same goes for relationships. Similar to the narrow highway is the narrowness of understanding and submission. You have to pay close attention to the spouse or significant other with whom you are on the highway of love.

You are two different people with different backgrounds and personalities, both traveling down this two-way street. The challenge comes with trying to live in harmony with one another without crossing that line of respect for another. You must understand that one false move or one wrong perception of the other could set you up for a head-on collision, with divorce or separation.

Crossed Lines

Too many relationships have been involved in head-on collisions, and instead of stopping to survey the scene to see where things went wrong, they keep on going. This is what you call "going through the motions." The people involved never took their hearts and minds to the body shop to get repaired.

Instead, they just keep on going with anger, strife, and hatred building up in their hearts, until eventually "out of nowhere," they lose it, they break down, and they leave. Out of the blue, they blurt out, "It's not working!"

What they really mean is, "I'm not working. I'm hurt, I'm damaged, and you don't care!" Can I tell you something? This didn't happen overnight. This didn't just come out of "nowhere." This can be dated back to a head-on collision on the highway of love.

Hit and Run

But it gets even deeper than that. Your significant other is the victim while you're the victor. You're guilty of committing a hit-and-run and fleeing the crime scene. You collided with your spouse, fled the scene, and didn't even look back to see how he or she was doing. Why? Because it's either your way or the highway! It's all about you. That's not how relationships work.

I know you might not have physically left, but emotionally and verbally, you have been gone for years. But can I tell you something? *You* did this. I promise you that you have contributed to this somehow, someway. You have to look into your heart and find out where you're contributing to the problem.

Search It Out

You need to turn around and revisit the crime scene. Where did you cross the line? When did you cross the line? What caused you to cross the line? Did you have to respond like that, even if your partner was wrong? What role are you playing in this madness?

Hear the Scripture now, and allow it to minister to you quietly. "Submit yourself *to one another*." Your partner may have some stuff that he or she needs to work on, but what do you need to work on? You just might be triggering the issue that he or she needs to work on. If you would handle your issue, maybe your partner wouldn't have one to bring to the table. You'll be amazed what happens when you begin to submit to one another in a relationship.

Listen Quick, Speak Slow

By your carnal nature, you naturally don't like backing down. You are overly aggressive in response and body language, which is causing "tilt" to be triggered in your spouse. Calm down. Humble yourself. You don't always have to get the last word in. There's a time to speak and a time to listen. I understand that you have an opinion, and Mama told you to "speak your mind," but use wisdom in that.

I understand what Mama said. But understand what James said, *"Be quick to listen, and slow to speak"* (James 1:19). You have to learn how to speak your mind at the right time. If things are already heated, you might just want to hold your comment and come back to it when things calm down. But when you leave the room, don't leave slamming doors; don't leave mumbling under your breath. God isn't getting any glory out of that.

Slow to Anger

God is glorified when you're quick to listen and when you think about how to answer. God is glorified when you're slow to speak and give the other person a chance to comment. But the latter part of that text says "slow to become angry." God is truly glorified when you can control your temper. How do I know? The Bible says, *"For man's anger does not bring about the righteous life that God desires"* (James 1:20).

It's not cool to blow up. It's not cool to lose it. It's not funny, cute, or acceptable. I didn't say it; God said it. That type of living doesn't bring forth the character that God desires, especially when you're doing it in front of your children. Don't become a stumbling block to your children because you can't manage your relationships and temper.

Open Your Heart

Submit yourself to one another. People may have some issues that need to be worked out, but where are you contributing to the problem? Maybe it's in your response. Maybe it's in your tone. Maybe it's in your gestures that continuously trigger others.

Imagine a relationship with two individuals yielding to one another instead of trying to change the other. You have to respect each other's points of view. Enjoy each other's differences. This is what makes you so unique and beautiful in the eyes of God. Stop being stuck in your ways and open your heart to others. You'll be amazed at the peace that it brings.

People are not perfect. But you must pinpoint where you're contributing to their issues and submit that area unto the Lord. Take heed to these principles. I promise they will turn your two-way street into a four-lane highway!

It's Me

It's me. It's me, Oh Lord, standing in the need of prayer.

Throughout these chapters I purposely took myself out of the equation and directed all the attention to you. I did this so that you wouldn't find comfort or cop-out with your issues. Many times we stop striving for better as long as someone else is struggling like we are.

Growing up, I remember going to class knowing that I didn't study for my test. I would ask my friend beside me, "Did you study for the test?" He would say no, and I would say, "Me either!" I would turn away from him feeling comfort that I wasn't alone—as if that made it okay.

First Partaker

I didn't want this mindset to hinder your examinations. For this cause, the Lord dealt strictly with you and removed me out the equation. But don't be fooled. The mailman may be delivering mail, but somebody is delivering his, too.

We all have mail, and we all have issues. And in order for me to effectively talk to you, the Lord had to first talk to me. I was the first partaker in this book long before it became a book. These corrections, rebukes, and words of encouragement are all real to me. This is why the words have been so passionate and heartfelt.

This Is My Story

What you have read is my story. What you have heard were my cries. What you have read were my weaknesses that left me saying, "It's me, Lord; it's me, standing in the need of prayer." While the Lord was waiting on others, He heard my humble cry. The Lord didn't pass me by. But when He came, I had to learn how to deal with myself.

For years I knew there was more to life than I had been accomplishing. I knew there was something that the Lord wanted me to do. I just couldn't grasp it. I couldn't obtain that standard that He was calling me to. I could see it, I could preach it—but I couldn't achieve it.

So what did I do? I did what most people do. I began to blame others. I began to lash out at those closest to me. I blamed them for my shortcomings, my setbacks, and my lack of achievements. They didn't know it, but I blamed them and scolded them internally. Hatred and anger began to build up inside me. I had to blame somebody. Somebody had to take the blame for my failures. It sure wasn't going to be me, so it had to be them!

Achan

Then one day, I allowed God to be God. The Lord sent the Holy Spirit in my life in the form of Nathan. He began to show me that I was looking everywhere but within. He began to show me that I had an Achan camping out within.

Achan was holding me back from conquering new territory in my life. I had buried some things that needed to be dealt with. I had buried some issues that needed to be brought to the frontline.

They needed to be stoned; they needed to be consumed by the fire of the Lord. They were holding me back. I began to understand that it wasn't them, and it wasn't my wife; I humbly whispered three words, "It's me, Lord." It was me standing in the need of prayer.

My problem was simple. I was *waiting* on others, I was *blaming* others, and I was *depending* on others. I was sitting around looking for handouts. I was sitting around waiting for somebody to feel sorry for me. I was sitting around blaming everyone, but never taking responsibility for myself.

My Nathan Moments

But one day, the Holy Spirit called me into His office and said, "Let's reason together. Though your sins and shortcomings are scarlet-red, I can make you white as snow. I can transform you, I can heal you, I can deliver you, and I can set you free. All I need you to do is one thing. Humble yourself under the mighty hand of God." That very hour, I humbled myself and began to accept responsibility for my life. I took the road less travelled on. I began dealing with Self.

Everything that I encouraged you to conquer, I had to conquer. I'm now occupying that territory for the Lord. I needed a Nathan in my life. I'm here to let you know that the Holy Spirit will be that Nathan for you, but you have to humble yourself to the truth and just admit it. Don't try to fight it.

In other areas of my life that I didn't want to budge, God had to send tangible Nathans in my life, the latter being my Pastor, Pastor Pierce, whom I thank God for. We would get around that table on Thursday nights with the men, and he would find me. It was there that I learned about my achilles heels. (my weakest areas)

It Was Me

I would comment on topics as if I had wisdom or insight, but he found my weaknesses through his teachings, and I thank God for that. He taught me the meaning of true submission. Pastor and Elder Pierce inspired me to look within. They confirmed that I was the problem, and for that, I'm eternally grateful.

Everything that I have spoken about to you here, I experienced firsthand—fear, insecurity, pride, and debt. This is my story; this is my song! I was the one who needed a new mind resolution. I was the one who couldn't get approved for a house because of bad credit and no savings.

But God!

I was the one who was feeding into the accuser of the brethren. I was the one that was puffed up; I was afraid of stepping out. I was the one who had poor eating habits. I was the one who didn't want to yield in my marriage. I didn't want to change, but I wanted my wife to change. That was my story; that was my song. But now I'm praising my Savior all day!

Pride, Humility, Honor

I'm praising my Savior because He looked past my faults, and He saw my needs. He delivered me from myself. He delivered me from my evil twin. I humbled myself before the Lord, and He exalted me in due season.

I stand before you today as a published author with three books written—two published—who was once afraid to step out into the deep!

I stand before you today as a joyful married man who hasn't argued with my wife in four and a half years, and we've been married for five. I submitted myself unto her, and low and behold, she submitted herself unto me. The two have become one, and God is glorified.

I got rid of the pride, and God saw fit for me to become a Minister of the Gospel. I got rid of the pride, and God saw fit to elevate me to State Youth Director of the Full Gospel Fellowship. I got rid of the pride, and God saw fit to promote me to Elder! I got rid of my insecurities, and I'm enjoying life. I'm enjoying my family. I'm enjoying my church. I'm enjoying my co-workers.

The Abundant Life

I dared myself to face *me*; look what God has done! Creditors aren't calling anymore, I've got change in the bank, and I'm established for the future. I'm not renting anymore! We purchased a brand new home—1600 square feet of beauty with three hefty rooms: *"The Lord heard my cry and he brought me into a spacious place"* (Psalms 119:5).

All of the above testimony started with two whispered words, "It's me." I had to yield; I had to submit. I had to let God be God. I had to deal with myself one-on-one. I had to stop blaming others and take a serious look in the mirror. All this time that I was telling you that it's you, it's only because I found victory when I said *it's me*. I desire for you to experience this victory as well!

God loves you, and He desires you to experience life more abundantly. God desires to bring out the best in you. All you have to do is **surrender** all to God. **Submit** to His ways and **commit** to His patterns and principles.

Start Here

Want to change but don't know how? It's simple. I want you to go somewhere nice and quiet. Be still, close your eyes, and softly whisper these words. Slowly say, "It's me; it's me, O Lord, standing in the need of prayer."

Humble yourself under the mighty hand of God, that he may exalt you in due time. 1 Peter 5:6

Acknowledgements

To the blessed Trinity: All glory, praise, and honor belong to you. Thank you for the creation, calling, and choosing of Albert Brooks Almore. I'm forever at your service.

To my good thing Pamela S. Almore: What else can I say but that I love you? Thank you for your understanding heart and willing hands. You are God-sent and my biggest supporter. Without you, none of this would be possible. Outside of Christ, you and Biship are my everything.

To my parents. I love you. All I want to do is make you proud. I praise God that you are alive and well to see the manifestation of your deposits. I could never repay you for all that you've done. But God can, and God will, in this lifetime and the lifetime to come. God bless you and thank you for your commitment to my life.

To my father- and mother-in-law, Greg and Stephanie Simmons. Thank you for all that you have done, all that you do, and all that you're going to do. I'm blessed to have in-laws such as you. You've been a blessing in so many ways. All I can say is thank you, and I love you.

To Pastor and Elder Pierce and my St. John Church Family: Thank you for embracing my family and me with such love and support. Keep the love, fellowship, and FOOD coming! God bless you!

To you, you, and you: If you're holding this book, I want to thank you for your inspiration. To all my family, friends, and supporters, each of you has played a significant part to help develop me into the man of God I am today. Continue allowing God to use you, and in return, I will do the same.

Other books by Albert B. Almore

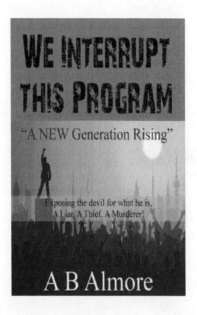

We Interrupt This Program is a raw book for a raw generation. This book is a must-have for youth, young adults, and youth leaders! It is equipped with understanding of the times, and it focuses on exposing the enemy. Children who didn't even like to read have reported reading this book as many as three times. With chapters such as "Jesus Was a Virgin," "The Club Vs. The Church," "I Lust You," and "Sex Is a Weapon," it's no wonder why so many churches have incorporated these teachings in their youth groups. This book will strengthen any youth and young adult in their Christian walk with Christ. It will help any youth leaders, parents, or guardians who are having a hard time connecting with a youth or with their very own child. *We Interrupt This Program* is the answer to today's times!

For Book Orders or Speaking Engagements:

St. John MB Church
Overseer John H. Pierce, Jr., Pastor

1130 Walt Bellamy Drive

New Bern, North Carolina 28562

252.638.6910

stjohnmb@embarqmail.com

www.abalmore.com

Elder Albert B. Almore is the Youth Director at St. John Missionary Baptist Church under the leadership of Overseer John H. Pierce. He also serves as the State Youth Director of the North Carolina Full Gospel Baptist Church Fellowship. He speaks life to all ages and enjoys bringing out the best in everyone. For more information please visit www.abalmore.com.

Made in the USA
Charleston, SC
03 September 2010